Teach Yourself

Practical Music Theory for All Guitarists

ROGER EDISON

Alfred Publishing Co., Inc.
16320 Roscoe Blvd., Suite 100
P.O. Box 10003
Van Nuys, CA 91410-0003
alfred.com

ISBN-10: 0-88284-688-4
ISBN-13: 978-0-88284-688-0

Cover photographs: Martin D-28 courtesy of the Martin Guitar Company
Fender Stratocaster courtesy of Fender Musical Instruments, Inc.

CONTENTS

TYPES OF GUITARS

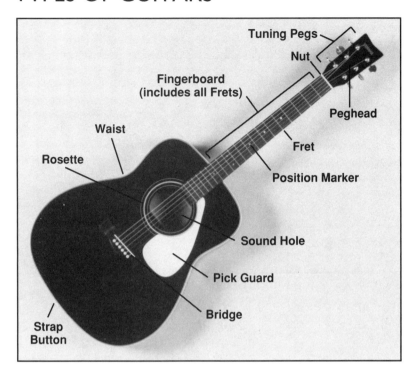

Acoustic Flat Top Guitar

Acoustic Flat Top guitars have narrow necks and steel strings. They are either strummed with a flat pick or played with one or more finger picks. They are used in rock, blues, country and folk playing.

Strings: Steel
Gauge: Light or Medium

Solid Body Electric Guitar

Solid body electrics have narrow necks, light-gauge strings and one or more electrical pickups. The output of these pickups is fed through an amplifier and is sometimes modified further by using wah-wah pedals, distortion pedals, choruses or other means of altering the tone. Solid body electrics are used almost exclusively for rock, heavy metal, blues, country and jazz music.

Strings: Steel
Gauge: Light

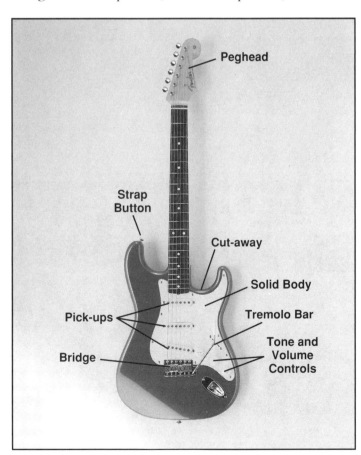

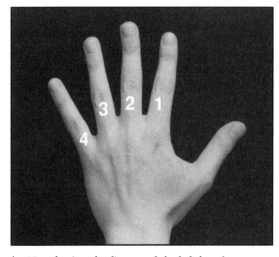

▲ *Numbering the fingers of the left hand.*

ACOUSTICS FOR GUITAR

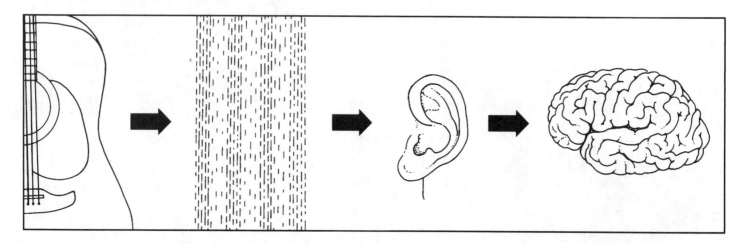

The word "acoustics" refers to the way sounds are produced. It is important to remember that all sounds, not only musical ones, are perceived by the human ear from the detection of sound waves. For a sound to be heard, three things must be present:

1. The generator. This is the thing that causes the vibration. In the case of the guitar, the generator is the guitar string.

2. The transmitting medium. In order for the sound to reach the ear, it must travel through the air, water, or even a solid object like a wall.

3. The receiver (the eardrum). This is a tightly stretched membrane inside the ear that vibrates when sound waves strike it. The vibration is then communicated to the brain.

Air is made up of innumerable particles of gases including oxygen, nitrogen and carbon dioxide. When a guitar string vibrates back and forth it causes the molecules of gas to compress in heavier concentrations, with thinner concentrations in between. These waves move through the air much like ocean waves move through water. When they strike the eardrum it makes that organ vibrate back and forth at the same speed as the guitar string. These vibrations are then translated by the brain into the sensation of sound.

VIBRATION

Guitar strings can be made to vibrate in several different ways. The two main ones are with a pick and with the fingertips.

Other methods used are strumming with the thumb, using finger picks, frailing (using the fingernails of the right hand to strike the strings) and hammering down on the strings with the thumb or fingers of either hand.

▲ *Pick strikes string and causes it to vibrate*

▲ *Fingertip strikes string and causes it to vibrate*

PITCH

Pitch is the word musicians use when they want to refer to how high or low a sound is. Pitch is caused by vibration. Faster vibration causes higher pitch. Slower vibration causes lower pitch. For example, a note that vibrates at 440 vibrations per second (vps) is perceived by the ear to be higher than a note that vibrates at 220vps, and lower than a note that vibrates at 880vps. Most people can hear low notes that vibrate as slowly as 20vps. High notes can be heard up to 15,000 or even 20,000 vps. Certain animals, especially dogs, can hear much higher than even these notes. The lowest string on a guitar vibrates at 82.5vps, the highest at 330vps.

On the guitar there are three ways to change the pitch of a string:

1. Turning the tuning or machine head (see drawing on page 3) causes the string to become tighter or looser. Tighter makes the pitch rise. Looser makes the pitch drop.

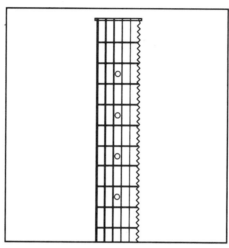

◀ *String vibrates for its full length. Make note of the pitch.*

2. Placing a finger of the left hand on any fret of a string effectively shortens the length of that string. As the finger slides closer to the bridge, the string length gets shorter and the pitch rises. Shorter makes the pitch rise. Longer makes the pitch drop.

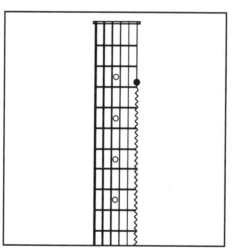

▲ *Finger on 3rd fret. String is shortened and the pitch rises.*

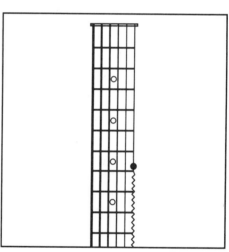

▲ *Finger is on 7th fret. String is short-ened even more and the pitch rises further.*

3. Pushing or bending a string across the fingerboard increases the string's tension even more and causes the pitch to rise. This effect is often used by blues and rock players.

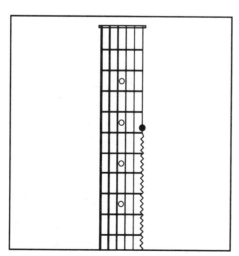

▲ *Fretted string vibrates at 440vps.*

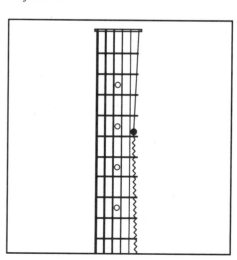

▲ *String is pushed or bent across finger board. Tension is increased and pitch rises.*

NOTES

Notes are the basic units of music. To play a note on the guitar, play any string and let it vibrate. Or, place a left hand finger on a fret and strike the string; let it vibrate.

Written music tells you what note to play by placing an oval shape on a five-line staff.

In music, notes are named by the letters A, B, C, D, E, F and G. No other letters are used.

In order to identify the notes on the five-line staff, a symbol called a **clef** is placed at the beginning of each staff. Music for the guitar is written in the **treble clef** which looks like this:

The treble clef symbol is derived from the Gothic letter G:

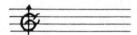

The modern clef still shows the position of the note G by curling around the second line of the staff, the place where G is written.

Bar lines are vertical lines that divide the staff into **measures**. This shows the basic pulse of the music and makes reading music easier by dividing the notes into shorter groups.

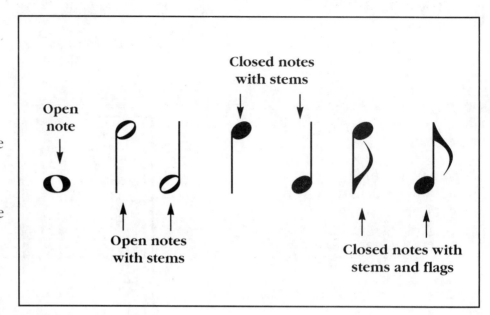

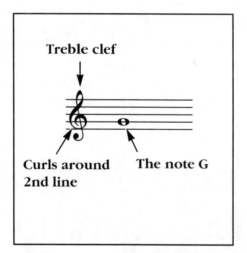

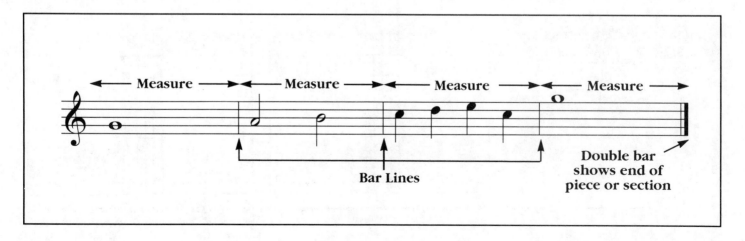

NAMING THE NOTES

Notes are placed on the five-line staff either in the spaces or on the lines.

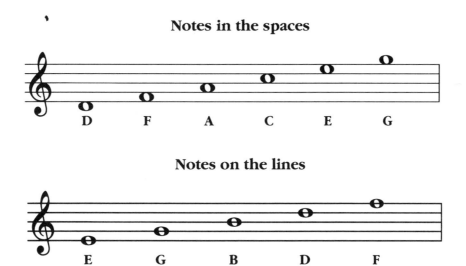

The following memory tricks will help you identify the notes:

In the spaces: **D**on't **F**orget, **A**ll **C**hildren **E**at **G**oodies

On the lines: **E**very **G**ood **B**oy **D**oes **F**ine

Identify the following notes and write their names in the spaces provided below each staff.

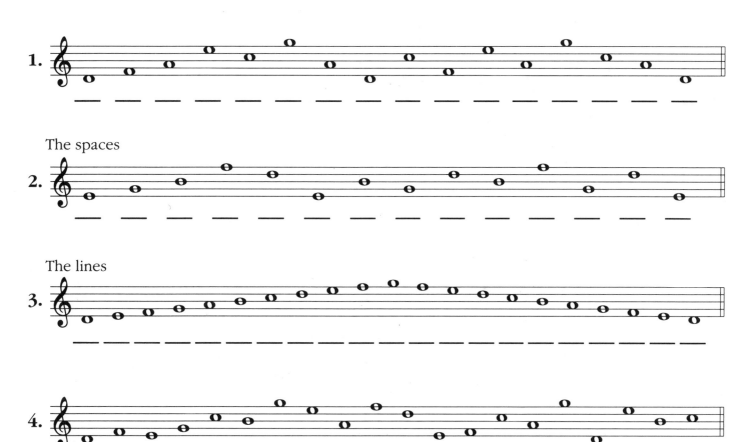

RIDDLES AND PUZZLES

1. What did Mary buy to go with her sequined dress?

2. What was the sheriff wearing after ten years in the desert?

3. What did Johnny take to get to Carnegie Hall?

4. But he didn't enjoy the concert.
A head cold made him _____.

5. A description of Darth Vader.

6. Sally shouldn't have told Gabriel her secret. Why?

A Limerick

There was a smart
monkey whose

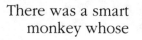

was very
hard to

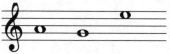

He had an old

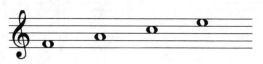

but could
swing like an

from the bottom to the top of his

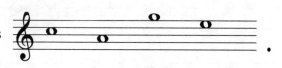

For answers, see page 60.

RHYTHM: QUARTER, HALF, DOTTED HALF AND WHOLE NOTES

As we have seen, the pitch of a note (how high or low it is) is indicated by its position on the five-line staff. The duration of a note (how long it sounds) is indicated by its shape.
Imagine a steady beat, like an army marching or a clock

ticking. Tap your foot to this beat. Now play any open string on the guitar once for each beat. These notes are called **quarter notes** and look like this: ♩ or ♪

Half notes get two beats and look like this: ♩ or ♪

Dotted half notes get three beats and look like this: ♩. or ♪.

Whole notes get four beats and look like this: o

Play the following exercises on open strings.

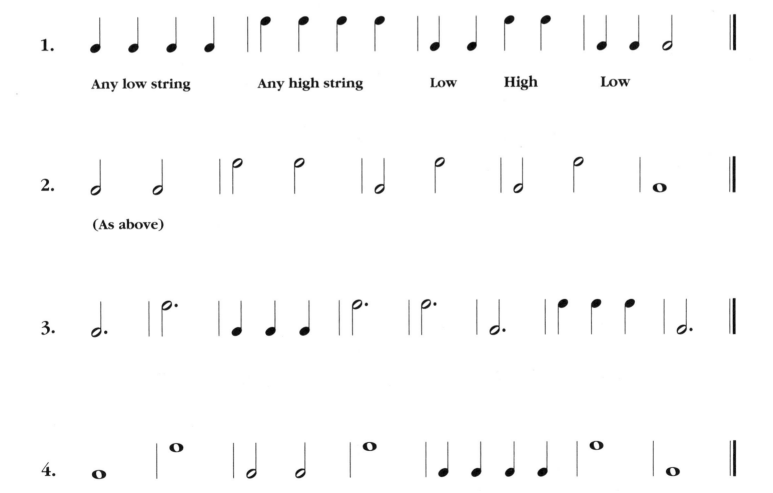

METER: MEASURES AND TIME SIGNATURES

Music is divided into **measures** of equal numbers of beats. At the beginning of each piece of music you'll find a fraction called a **time signature**. The upper number of the fraction tells you how many beats are contained within each measure. For example, a measure in 4/4 time (four quarter time) always contains four beats. Here are a few possibilities:

Notice that in the above example each measure adds up to four beats.

A measure in 3/4 (three quarter time) always adds up to three beats.

A measure in 2/4 (two quarter time) always up to two beats.

In the examples below, some beats have been omitted. Fill them in and complete the measures. (There are several correct answers.)

1.

2.

3.
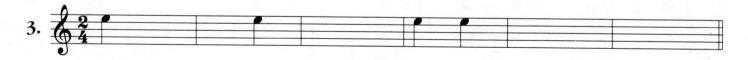

For answers, see page 60.

CHORDS

A **chord** is a group of three or more notes blended together. On guitar, chords are ordinarily used to accompany the singing voice or a melody played on another instrument. Chords are also used in solo guitar playing to enhance the melody and make it sound richer and fuller.

Chords are named for their most important note, called the **root**. The root of a C chord is the note C. The root of a G chord is the note G, and so on.

Although there are dozens of different types of chords used in today's music, the most widely used are just three: major, minor and seventh.

Below are three simple chords that are easy to play on the guitar. **o** means play the open string (do not finger), **X** means do not play the string.

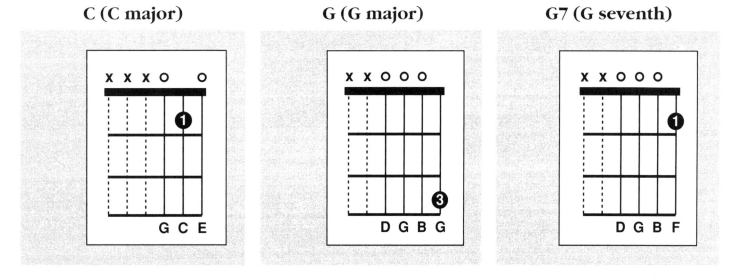

C (C major)	G (G major)	G7 (G seventh)
Contains the notes C, E and G	Contains the notes G, B and D	Contains the notes G, B, D and F

As you can see from the above, the notes do not necessarily appear in order. Also, sometimes a note appears twice.

RESTS: QUARTER, HALF AND WHOLE RESTS

When silence is called for in music, a symbol called a **rest** is used. It is important to remember that a rest is a measured silence, that is, a silence that lasts for a certain number of beats.

The rests used in music are:

Quarter rest ↥ = 1 beat of silence

Half rest ▬ = 2 beats of silence

(used only in 4/4 time)

Whole rest

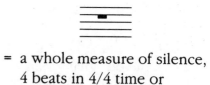

= a whole measure of silence, 4 beats in 4/4 time or 3 beats in 3/4 time or 2 beats in 2/4 time.

Play the following examples on the open 1st string. When you see a rest, stop the vibration of the string with the "heel" of the right hand.

Fill in the missing beats with the appropriate rest or rests. Remember, the half rest is used only in 4/4 time. In 3/4 time, use two quarter rests.

For answers, see page 60.

EXTENDING THE STAFF: LEGER LINES

Since the guitar can play notes that are both lower and higher than those which can be written on the staff, it is sometimes necessary to extend the five lines of the staff with short, temporary lines called **leger lines**.

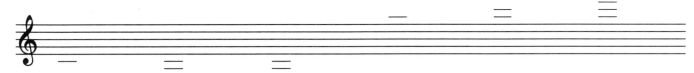

Leger lines above the staff

Leger lines below the staff

As with the normal staff, notes can be written either on the lines or in the spaces.

Here are the notes below the staff that are playable on the guitar:

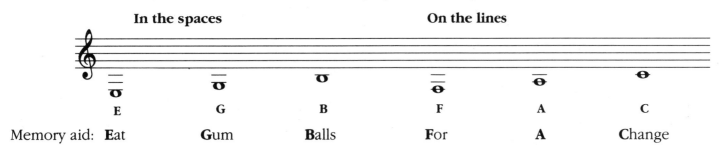

In the spaces			**On the lines**		
E	G	B	F	A	C

Memory aid: **Eat** **Gum** **Balls** **For** **A** **Change**

Or, think of a continuous sequence of notes in the spaces and on the lines.

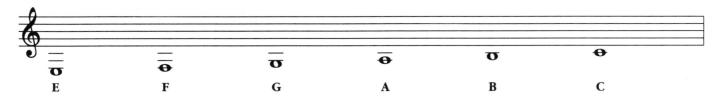

E	F	G	A	B	C

For now, we'll use only three notes above the staff. They're as simple as

A   B   C

SCALES: THE C MAJOR SCALE

A **scale** is a sequence of notes played in order. No letter name is skipped and none is repeated until the last note of the scale.

The **C major scale** starts and ends on the note C. It consists of the notes C, D, E, F, G, A, B and C.

Play this C major scale both ascending and descending:

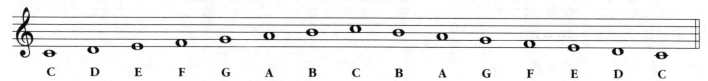

C   D   E   F   G   A   B   C   B   A   G   F   E   D   C

We can also start the C major scale on the higher note C and continue up from there:

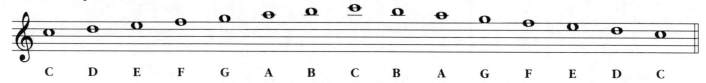

C   D   E   F   G   A   B   C   B   A   G   F   E   D   C

Or, the two scales can be played as one continuous scale from low to high and back again:

Although some people think that scales are boring, it is very important to practice them for many reasons:

1. To develop speed and facility on the fingerboard.

2. To learn the notes in a key. The notes in the key of C are all contained in the C major scale. Therefore, if you know the scale, you'll have a much easier time playing in the key.

3. To gain facility with melodic passages that are based on scales. For example, look at this excerpt from "Dixie":

⌐ **Part of the C major scale** ⌐

4. To learn how chords are built.

THREE PRINCIPAL CHORDS IN THE KEY OF C MAJOR

Three basic chords can be derived from every scale. With these three chords you can accompany most children's songs, folk songs, blues songs and many other simple songs. Here's how to find the basic three chords in the key of C major.

Start with the extended C major scale:

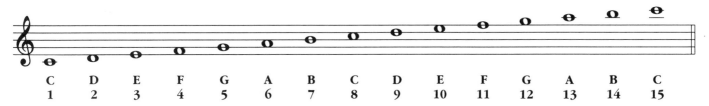

C	D	E	F	G	A	B	C	D	E	F	G	A	B	C
1	2	3	4	5	6	7	8	9	10	11	12	13	14	15

The most important chord in any key is called the I (one) chord. It consists of the 1, 3 and 5 notes of the scale. Looking at the C major scale above, you'll see that the I chord consists of the notes C (1), E (3) and G (5). This is called a C major chord.

The next most important chord is called the V7 (five-seven) chord. It consists of the 5, 7, 9 and 11 notes of the scale. Looking at the C major scale above, you'll see that the V7 chord consists of the notes G (5), B (7), D (9) and F (11). This is called a G7 (G seventh) chord.

Even using only the C and G7 chords discussed above, you can accompany many simple songs such as "Frère Jacques" and "Polly-Wolly-Doodle."

The third important chord in any key is called the IV (four) chord. It consists of the 4, 6 and 8 notes of the scale. Looking at the scale above, you'll see that the IV chord consists of the notes F (4), A (6) and C (8). This is called an F major chord.

With these three chords, C, F and G7, you can accompany thousands of songs that are in the key of C major.

SUMMARY

In the key of C major, the three principal chords are:

The I chord, C major, consisting of the notes C, E and G;

The IV chord, F major, consisting of the notes F, A and C;

The V7 chord, G seventh, consisting of the notes G, B, D and F.

PLAYING WITH CHORDS

On the guitar it is often necessary to play the notes of a chord in a
mixed-up order, to repeat a note or to omit a note.
Here are examples of three-note chords:

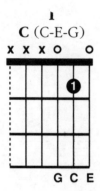

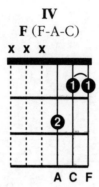

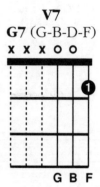

Here are examples of four-note chords:

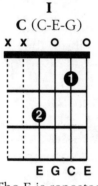

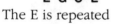

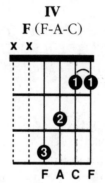

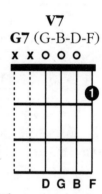

The notes of a chord can be played simultaneously.

The notes of a chord can be played one at a time.

The notes of a chord can be mixed in various ways.

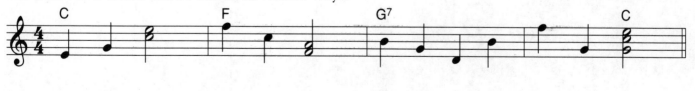

CHORD REVIEW

Name the following chords. Write the name above the staff:

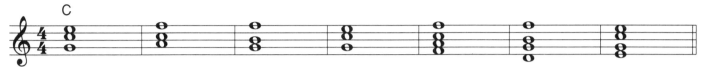

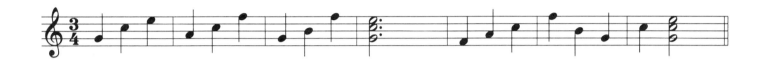

Write out different versions of the C chord, both simultaneously and with the notes played one at a time.

Write out different versions of the F chord.

Write out different versions of the G7 chord.

Play the following exercises based on the C, F and G7 chords.

This symbol means repeat the preceding chord.

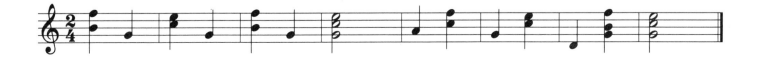

PICKUPS

Sometimes a song or other piece of music begins with an incomplete measure called a **pickup**. In 4/4 time the pickup can be one, two or three beats. Often, the last measure will be missing the same number of beats that the pickup uses. In this way the initial incomplete measure is completed.

Here are some short excerpts of familiar tunes showing pickups of various numbers of beats in 4/4 and 3/4 time.

Jimmy Crack Corn

When   I   was   young   I   used   to   wait   on   mas - ter   and   give   him   his   plate . . .

Red River Valley

From   this   val - ley   they   say   you   are   go   -   ing . . .

The Saints

Oh   when   the   saints   go   march - ing   in . . .

The Beautiful Blue Danube

Cowboy Jack

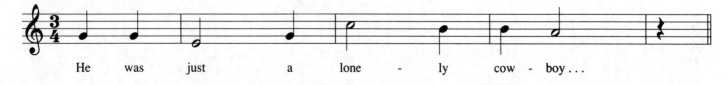

He   was   just   a   lone   -   ly   cow - boy . . .

TIES

A **tie** is symbolized by a curved line that connects two or more notes of the same pitch. When two notes are tied, the second one is not played separately. Rather, its value is added to the first note. For example, two tied quarter notes would be held for two beats. A half note tied to a quarter note would be held for three beats, and so on.

Here are various examples of tied notes in 4/4, 3/4, and 2/4 time. Play them on the open E string.

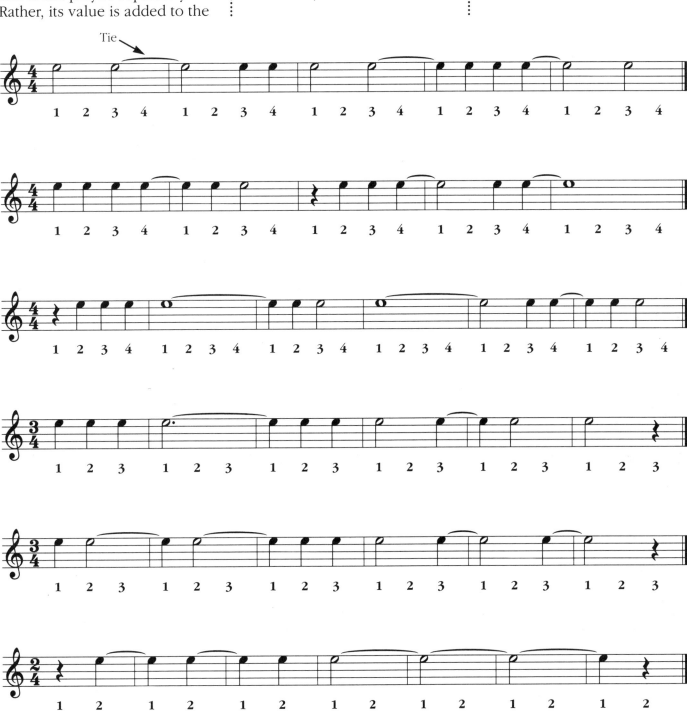

USING CHORDS TO ACCOMPANY SONGS

Use the chords you have learned to accompany the simple song below. Sing the melody as you strum four chords for each measure of music. Or, a friend can play the melody on some other instrument as you strum the chords.

Twinkle, Twinkle, Little Star

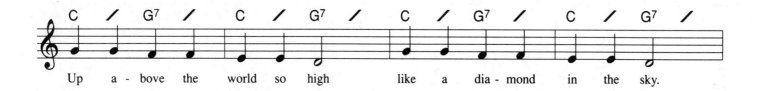

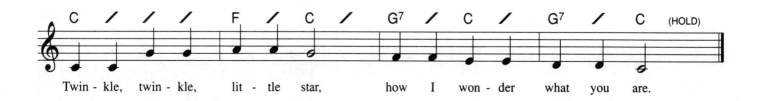

This is the simplest type of accompaniment. In 4/4 time, strum four times for each measure of music; in 3/4 time, strum three times for each measure.

Substituting a **bass note** for the first chord of every measure makes the accompaniment more interesting. The best bass note to use is the **root** of the chord. Remember, the root is the note that names the chord. For example, the root of a C chord is the (low) note C; the root of a G7 chord is the (low) note G, and so on. In general, it sounds best if you use the lowest note in the chord as the bass note.

Try "Twinkle, Twinkle, Little Star" again, this time substituting the bass note C, G or F for the first chord in each measure.

EIGHTH NOTES

Eighth notes look like ♪ or ♪ when they stand alone. When they are written in groups of two or more they look like this:

Eighth notes are played twice as fast as quarter notes. On guitar, pairs of eighth notes are usually played with down- and up-picks. The symbol for down-pick is ⊓.

For up-pick we use ∨. Make sure you can play the first line accurately before playing the rest of this page on the open 1st string.

NOTE FINDER REVIEW

Here are all the notes discussed in the book up to this point. Make sure you can name and play every note. Then cover the first line and see if you can name and play the notes on the rest of the page.

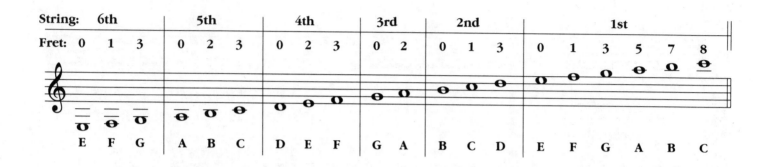

String:	6th			5th			4th			3rd		2nd			1st					
Fret:	0	1	3	0	2	3	0	2	3	0	2	0	1	3	0	1	3	5	7	8
	E	F	G	A	B	C	D	E	F	G	A	B	C	D	E	F	G	A	B	C

HALF STEPS AND WHOLE STEPS

A **half step** is the smallest difference in pitch that can be notated in music. On the guitar, a half step equals one fret. For example, the note E is played on the 4th string, 2nd fret. A half step above E is the note F, played on the 4th string, 3rd fret. Another example: The note C is played on the 5th string, 3rd fret. A half step below C is the note B, played on the 5th string, 2nd fret.

Describe by string and fret where to find the notes that are a half step above the following notes:

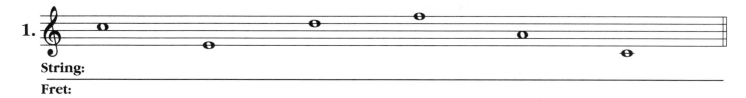

String:

Fret:

Describe by string and fret where to find the notes that are a half step below the following notes:

String:

Fret:

A **whole step** equals two half steps. A whole step on the guitar equals two frets. Any note a whole step higher than a given note is found two frets higher. Any note a whole step lower is found two frets lower.

Describe where to find the notes a whole step above the following notes:

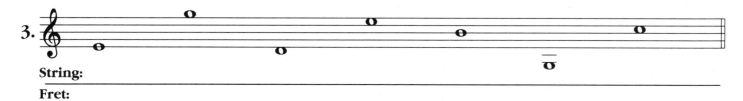

String:

Fret:

Describe where to find the notes a whole step below the following notes:

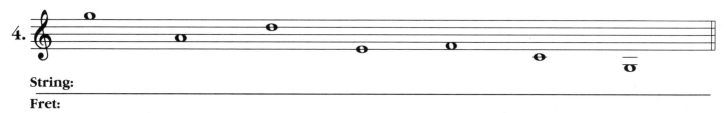

String:

Fret:

For answers, see page 60.

SHARPS AND NATURALS

The symbol ♯ is used to indicate a **sharp**. When placed in front of a note it means to play that note a half step (one fret) *higher* than usual. For example, if the note

G is played on the 6th string, 3rd fret, the note G♯ is played on the 6th string, 4th fret. If the note D is played on the open 4th string,

the note D♯ is played on the 4th string, 1st fret. Each of the notes below is shown both in its usual position and sharped. Fill in where to find the sharped note.

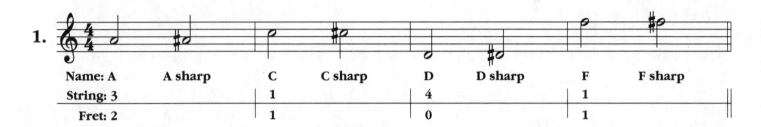

Name:	A	A sharp	C	C sharp	D	D sharp	F	F sharp
String:	3		1		4		1	
Fret:	2		1		0		1	

Name:	G	G sharp	C	C sharp	G	G sharp	G	G sharp
String:	3		5		6		1	
Fret:	0		3		3		3	

A **natural** symbol looks like ♮. When placed in front of a previously sharped note, it restores that note to its usual

position. If F♯ is played on the 4th string, 4th fret, F♮ is played on the 4th string, 3rd fret, and so on.

Each of the notes below is first shown sharped, then in its natural position. Fill in where to find the natural note.

Name:	D sharp	D natural	D sharp	D natural	A sharp	A natural	F sharp	F natural
String:	2		4		1		4	
Fret:	4		1		6		4	

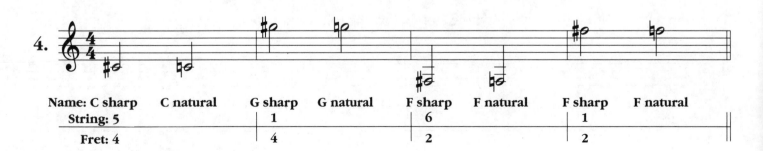

Name:	C sharp	C natural	G sharp	G natural	F sharp	F natural	F sharp	F natural
String:	5		1		6		1	
Fret:	4		4		2		2	

For answers, see page 60.

FLATS AND NATURALS

The symbol ♭ is used to indicate a **flat**. When placed in front of a note it means to play that note a half step (one fret) *lower* than usual. For example, if the note G is played on the 1st or 6th string, 3rd fret, the note G♭ is played on the 1st or 6th string, 2nd fret. If the note E is played on the 4th string, 2nd fret, the note E♭ is played on the 4th string, 1st fret, and so on.

Each of the notes below is shown both in its usual position and flatted. Fill in where to find the flatted note.

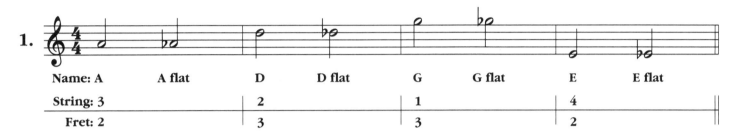

Name: A	A flat	D	D flat	G	G flat	E	E flat
String: 3		2		1		4	
Fret: 2		3		3		2	

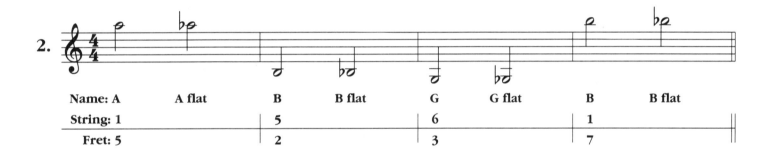

Name: A	A flat	B	B flat	G	G flat	B	B flat
String: 1		5		6		1	
Fret: 5		2		3		7	

As with sharps, a natural restores a flatted note to its usual position.

Each of the notes below is first shown flatted, then in its natural position. Fill in where to find the natural note.

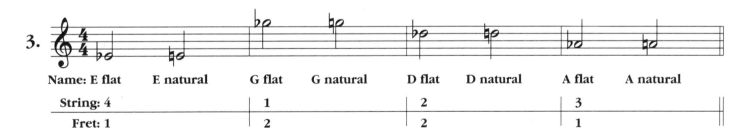

Name: E flat	E natural	G flat	G natural	D flat	D natural	A flat	A natural
String: 4		1		2		3	
Fret: 1		2		2		1	

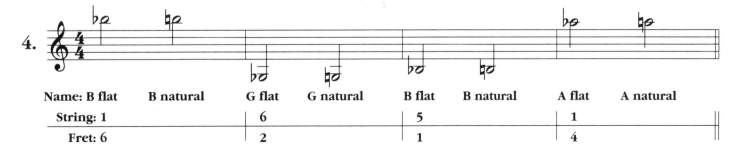

Name: B flat	B natural	G flat	G natural	B flat	B natural	A flat	A natural
String: 1		6		5		1	
Fret: 6		2		1		4	

For answers, see page 60.

HOW TO FLAT OPEN STRINGS

Since it is impossible to find the flat of an open string note on that string, you must find it on the next lower string. Here's how to flat the open E (1st) string:

First, find the note E on the next lower string, the 2nd string. E can be played on the 2nd string, 5th fret. This note can then be lowered to E♭, played on the 2nd string, 4th fret.

Study and play the following exercises. They explain how to flat every possible open string note on the guitar.

Name:	E	E	E flat		B	B	B flat		G	G	G flat		D	D	D flat		A	A	A flat
String:	1	2	2		2	3	3		3	4	4		4	5	5		5	6	6
Fret:	0	5	4		0	4	3		0	5	4		0	5	4		0	5	4

Here are all the flatted notes learned thus far. Write in their names and where to find them on the fingerboard.

1.
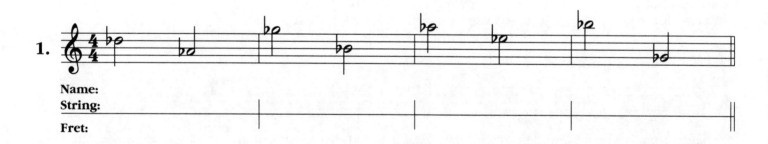

Name:

String:

Fret:

2.

Name:

String:

Fret:

For answers, see page 61.

ENHARMONICS

You may have already noticed that certain places on the fingerboard can be named two different ways. For example, the 1st string, 2nd fret can be called either F♯ or G♭. The 4th string, 1st fret is either D♯ or E♭, and so on. These are called **enharmonic tones** or simply **enharmonics**.

Here are some sharp notes. Write in the enharmonic flat in the space provided.

Here are some flat notes. Write in the enharmonic sharp in the space provided.

Some enharmonics make use of natural notes as well. For example, E♯ is the same as F. B♯ is the same as C. C♭ is the same as B. F♭ is the same as E. Although these are not used much, the serious student should understand and be able to play these notes.

For answers, see page 61.

THE CHROMATIC WHEEL

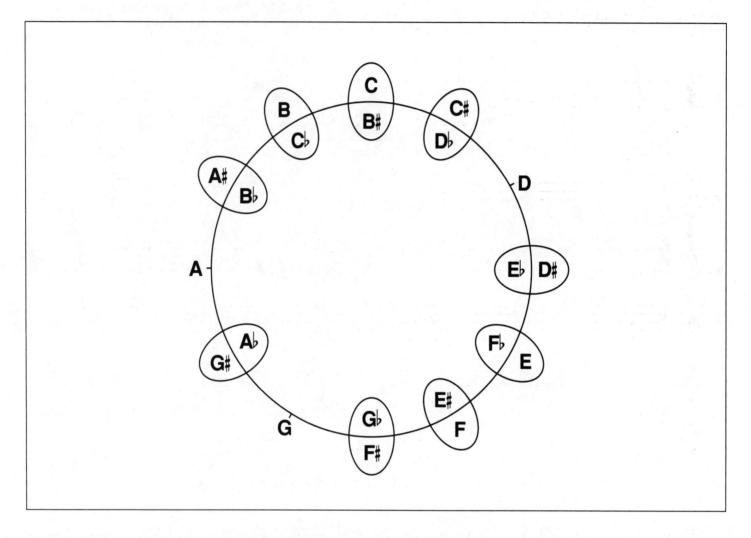

This useful chart shows you several things:

1. All enharmonic tones are linked within the ovals.

2. To find a half step above any note, find the note on the wheel and move one step clockwise. Example: A half step higher than F is F♯ or G♭.

3. To find a half step below any note, find the note on the wheel and move one position counterclockwise. Example: A half step lower than A is G♯ or A♭.

4. To find a whole step above any note, move two positions on the wheel in a clockwise direction. Example: A whole step above D♭ or C♯ is E♭ or D♯.

5. To find a whole step below any note, move two positions on the wheel in a counterclockwise direction. Example: A whole step below G is F or E♯.

HALF STEP AND WHOLE STEP QUIZ

Write a half note that is a *half step higher* than each half note below. Sometimes there are several correct answers. For example, in the first measure, the answer is either E# or F.

Write a half note that is a *half step lower* than each half note below.

Write a half note that is a *whole step higher* than each half note below.

Write a half note that is a *whole step lower* than each half note below.

For answers, see page 61.

MAJOR SCALES

Before starting this page, review the material on page 14. The C major scale consists of the notes C, D, E, F, G, A, B and C. If we analyze the distance between the notes in the scale, we find a particular pattern of half steps and whole steps.

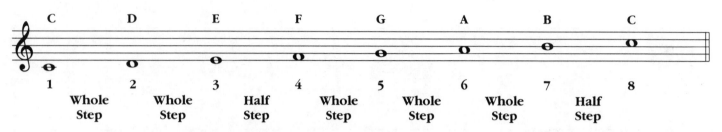

You can see from the above that each note in the C major scale is a whole step away from its neighbor except for the 3rd and 4th steps (E to F) and the 7th and 8th steps (B to C); these are a half step away. A shorthand way to remember this is whole, whole, half, whole, whole, whole, half or, simply, 2½, 3½. **Every major scale must conform to this pattern.**

Here are some sequences of eight notes. Write in the space below the distance from each note to the next note. Are any of the sequences below major scales?

For answers, see page 61.

BUILDING THE G MAJOR SCALE

First, write the notes from G to G without skipping or repeating any letter.

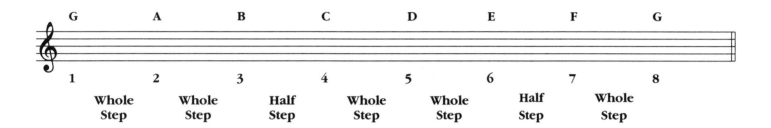

Next, check each interval in the scale to make sure that it conforms to the pattern of half steps and whole steps that define a major scale. Do it like this:

From the 1st to the 2nd step should be a whole step; it is.

From the 2nd to the 3rd step should be a whole step; it is.

From the 3rd to the 4th step should be a half step; it is.

From the 4th to the 5th step should be a whole step; it is.

From the 5th to the 6th step should be a whole step; it is.

From the 6th to the 7th step should be a whole step; it is not. From E to F is a half step. Therefore, the F must be raised for it to be farther from the E. We can do this by **sharping the F**. Once this is done, the distance from E to F♯ is a whole step.

From the (new) 7th step (F♯) to the 8th step (G) should be a half step; it is. And this completes the G major scale.

Correct form of the G Major Scale

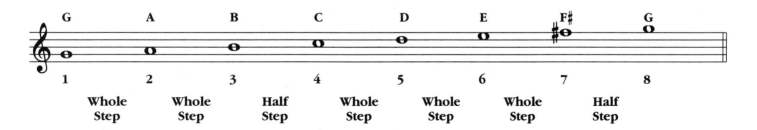

THE THREE PRINCIPAL CHORDS IN THE KEY OF G MAJOR

As you learned on page 15, the three principal chords in any key are the I, IV and V7. Now that you know the G major scale, you can derive the three principal chords in the key of G major.

Start with a two-octave G major scale:

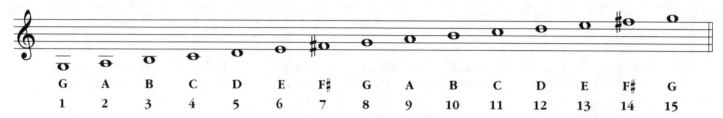

G	A	B	C	D	E	F♯	G	A	B	C	D	E	F♯	G
1	2	3	4	5	6	7	8	9	10	11	12	13	14	15

The I chord consists of the 1, 3 and 5 notes of the scale. Looking at the G major scale above, you'll see that the I chord consists of the notes G (1), B (3) and D (5). This is called a G major chord.

The IV chord consists of the 4, 6 and 8 notes of the scale. Look-ing at the scale above, you'll see that the IV chord consists of the notes C (4), E (6) and G (8). This is called a C major chord.

The V7 chord consists of the 5, 7, 9 and 11 notes of the scale. Looking at the G major scale above, you'll see that the V7 chord consists of the notes D (5), F♯ (7), A (9) and C (11). This is called a D seventh chord.

With these three chords, G, C and D7, you can accompany thousands of songs in the key of G major.

Here are easy forms of the three principal chords in the key of G major:

I
G (G-B-D)

G B D G B G

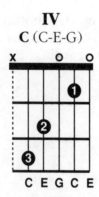

IV
C (C-E-G)

C E G C E

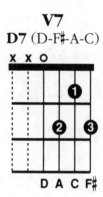

V7
D7 (D-F♯-A-C)

D A C F♯

SUMMARY

In the key of G major, the three principal chords are:

The I chord, G major, consisting of the notes G, B and D;

The IV chord, C major, consisting of the notes C, E and G;

The V7 chord, D seventh, consisting of the notes D, F♯, A and C.

BUILDING THE F MAJOR SCALE

First, write the notes from F to F without skipping or repeating any letter.

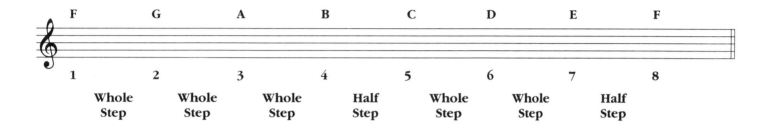

Next, check each interval in the scale to make sure that it conforms to the pattern of half steps and whole steps that define a major scale. Do it like this:

From the 1st to the 2nd step should be a whole step; it is.

From the 2nd to the 3rd step should be a whole step; it is.

From the 3rd to the 4th step should be a half step; it is not. From A to B is a whole step. Therefore, the B must be lowered to bring it closer to the A.

We can do this by flatting the B. Once this is done, the distance from A to B♭ is a half step.

From the (new) 4th step (B♭) to the 5th step should be a whole step; it is.

From the 5th to the 6th step should be a whole step; it is.

From the 6th to the 7th step should be a whole step; it is.

From the 7th to the 8th step should be a half step; it is. And this completes the F major scale.

Correct form of the F Major Scale

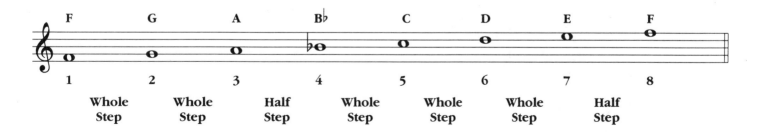

THE THREE PRINCIPAL CHORDS IN THE KEY OF F MAJOR

As you learned on page 15, the three principal chords in any key are the I, IV, and V7. Now that you know the F major scale, you can derive the three principal chords in the key of F major.

Start with a two-octave F major scale:

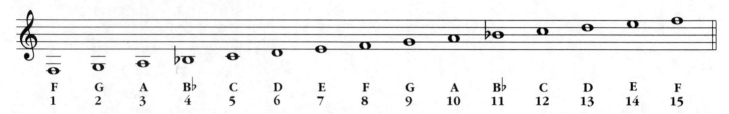

F	G	A	B♭	C	D	E	F	G	A	B♭	C	D	E	F
1	2	3	4	5	6	7	8	9	10	11	12	13	14	15

Remember, the I chord consists of the 1, 3 and 5 notes of the scale. Looking at the F major scale above, you'll see that the I chord consists of the notes F (1), A (3) and C (5). This is called an F major chord.

The IV chord consists of the 4, 6 and 8 notes of the scale. Using the scale above, you'll see that the IV chord consists of B♭ (4), D (6) and F (8). This is called a B♭ major chord.

The V7 chord consists of the 5, 7, 9 and 11 notes of the scale. Looking at the F major scale above, you'll see that the V7 chord consists of the notes C (5), E (7), G (9) and B♭ (11). This is called a C seventh chord.

With these three chords, F, B♭ and C7, you can accompany thousands of songs in the key of F major.

Here are the easiest forms of the three principal chords in the key of F major:

I	**IV**	**V7**
F (F-A-C)	B♭ (B♭-D-F)	C7 (C-E-G-B♭)

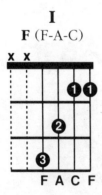

F A C F

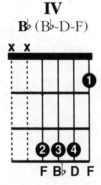

F B♭ D F

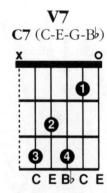

C E B♭ C E

(No G in this form of C7)

SUMMARY

In the key of F major, the three principal chords are:

The I chord, F major, consisting of the notes F, A and C;

The IV chord, B♭ major, consisting of the notes B♭, D and F;

The V7 chord, C seventh, consisting of the notes C, E, G and B♭.

KEY SIGNATURES IN THE KEYS OF
C MAJOR, F MAJOR AND G MAJOR

Summing up what we have learned on the last few pages, here are
the three major scales that we have discussed:

C Major Scale

G Major Scale

F Major Scale

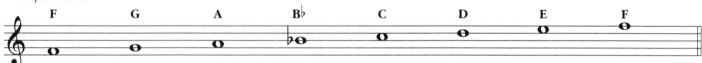

As you can see, the C major scale does not require either sharps or flats; the G major scale has an F♯; the F major scale has a B♭. In order to save writing in the sharps and flats when in the key of G or F, musicians use a **key signature**. This is one or more sharps or flats indicated at the beginning of each line of music. If no sharps or flats are placed there, it usually means that the piece is in the key of C major. Here then are the three scales as above, this time written using key signatures:

Key of C major (no sharps, no flats)

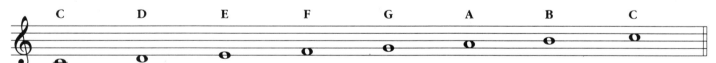

Key of G major (F is always played as F♯ unless preceded by a natural sign)

Key of F major (B is always played as B♭ unless preceded by a natural sign)

THE EIGHTH REST

The symbol 𝄾 is used to indicate an 8th rest. This symbol means to leave a silence the length of an 8th note, that is, a half beat.

When 8th notes appear singly they look like: ♪ or ♪.

Single 8th notes are often used with 8th rests: **Count: 1 & 2 &**

8th rests are also used with beamed 8th notes: 1 & 2 &

Clap or tap the following rhythm: **Count: 1 & 2 & 3 & 4 &   1 & 2 & 3 & 4 &**

On guitar, when playing a fingered note, the sound is cut off by releasing the pressure of the finger on the string. When playing an open string, the sound is cut off by touching the string either with a left hand finger or with the "heel" of the right hand.

Try playing the following:

Eighth rests may also appear on downbeats. This creates no unusual difficulty if you **mark the downbeat by tapping your foot** or counting mentally.

1 & 2 &   1 & 2 &   1 & 2 &   1 & 2 &

Practice the following rhythmic exercises on any string. Make sure to count accurately and to mark unplayed downbeats with a foot tap.

DOTTED QUARTER NOTES

Placing a dot after a note increases its value by half. For example, placing a dot after a half note (which is held for two beats) increases its value by half, so a dotted half note is held for three beats.

Placing a dot after a quarter note (which is held for one beat) increases its value by half, so a dotted quarter note is held for one-and-a-half beats.

The next two lines show two different ways of notating the same rhythm.

Here are some fragments of familiar tunes that use the dotted quarter rhythm:

All Through the Night

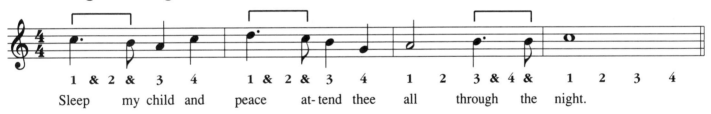

Green Grow the Lilacs

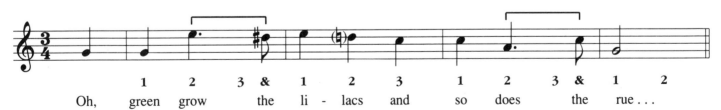

The Happy Farmer

INTERVALS
2nds, 3rds, 4ths, 5ths, 6ths, 7ths and 8vas

The space from any note to a different note is called an **interval**. Intervals are always figured by letter names. From any letter to the next letter, from C to D, for example, is called a **second**. Always count the first letter as "one." From any letter to two letters away, from D to F, for example, is called a **third**, and so on.

Here are examples of intervals in the key of C major:

*Intervals of the 8th are always referred to by their French name, *octave*, often abbreviated as 8va (plural is 8vas).

DRILL ON IDENTIFYING INTERVALS

Name the following intervals:

1. 2nd ___ ___ ___ ___ ___

2. ___ ___ ___ ___ ___ ___

3. ___ ___ ___ ___ ___ ___

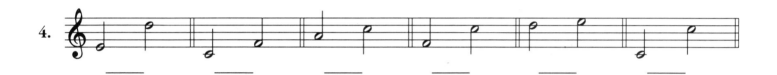

4. ___ ___ ___ ___ ___ ___

In each measure, fill in another note (ascending) that makes the interval correct:

5. 2nd 8va 3rd 7th 5th 4th

6. 6th 3rd 2nd 5th 5th 6th

7. 8va 2nd 6th 4th 7th 3rd

8. 5th 4th 7th 3rd 2nd 8va

For answers, see page 62.

INTERVALS IN THE KEYS OF F MAJOR AND G MAJOR

Since intervals are measured by letter names only, the addition of a sharp or flat in the key signature does not alter the name of the interval. Here are examples of intervals in the keys of F major and G major; identify them in the spaces below.

Key of F Major

2nd

Key of G Major

3rd

For answers, see page 62.

DERIVING MINOR CHORDS FROM THE MAJOR SCALE: THE II, III AND VI CHORDS

As you learned on page 15, the three principal chords in any key are the I, IV and V7. Other chords may also be derived from the major scale. These are the II, III and VI chords, and are based on the 2, 3 and 6 notes of the major scale respectively. Although the II, III and VI chords are not used as much as the I, IV and V7 chords, they are quite common and should be understood by every serious student.

The II, III and VI Chords in the Key of C Major

Start with a two-octave C major scale:

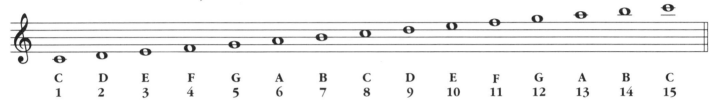

C	D	E	F	G	A	B	C	D	E	F	G	A	B	C
1	2	3	4	5	6	7	8	9	10	11	12	13	14	15

For the II chord, use the 2, 4 and 6 notes of the scale (D, F and A). This is called a D minor chord, often notated as Dm.

For the III chord, use the 3, 5 and 7 notes of the scale (E, G and B). This is called an E minor (Em) chord.

For the VI chord, use the 6, 8 and 10 notes of the scale (A, C and E). This is called an A minor (Am) chord.

Here are the easiest forms of the chords discussed above:

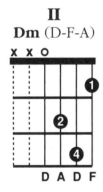

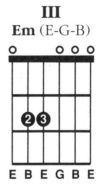

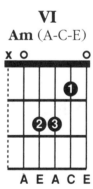

SUMMARY

The six most common chords in the key of C major are:

The I chord, C major, consisting of the notes C, E and G;

The II chord, D minor, consisting of the notes D, F and A;

The III chord, E minor, consisting of the notes E, G and B;

The IV chord, F major, consisting of the notes F, A and C;

The V7 chord, G seventh, consisting of the notes G, B, D and F;

The VI chord, A minor, consisting of the notes A, C, and E.

THE II, III AND VI CHORDS IN THE KEY OF F MAJOR

Start with a two-octave F major scale:

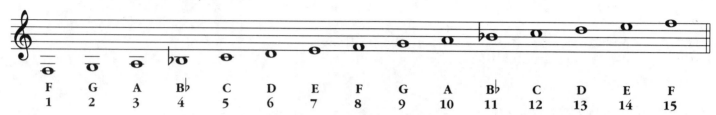

F	G	A	B♭	C	D	E	F	G	A	B♭	C	D	E	F
1	2	3	4	5	6	7	8	9	10	11	12	13	14	15

For the II chord, use the 2, 4 and 6 notes of the scale (G, B♭ and D). This is called a G minor (Gm) chord.

For the III chord, use the 3, 5 and 7 notes of the scale (A, C and E). This is called an A minor (Am) chord.

For the VI chord, use 6, 8 and 10 notes of the scale (D, F and A). This is called a D minor (Dm) chord.

Here are the easiest forms of the chords discussed above:

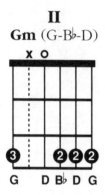

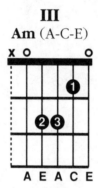

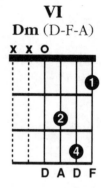

SUMMARY

The six most common chords in the key of F major are:

The I chord, F major, consisting of the notes F, A and C;

The II chord, G minor, consisting of the notes G, B♭ and D;

The III chord, A minor, consisting of the notes A, C and E;

The IV chord, B♭ major, consisting of the notes B♭, D and F;

The V7 chord, C seventh, consisting of the notes C, E, G and B♭;

The VI chord, D minor, consisting of the notes D, F and A.

Note: You'll notice that chords can have different functions, depending on the key. For example, the F major chord is the IV chord in the key of C major and the I chord in the key of F major. The D minor chord is the II chord in the key of C major and the VI chord in the key of F major, and so on.

THE II, III AND VI CHORDS IN THE KEY OF G MAJOR

Start with a two-octave G major scale:

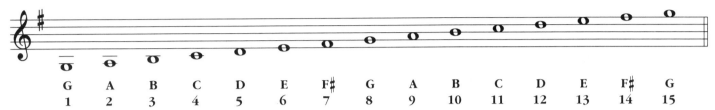

G	A	B	C	D	E	F♯	G	A	B	C	D	E	F♯	G
1	2	3	4	5	6	7	8	9	10	11	12	13	14	15

For the II chord, use the 2, 4 and 6 notes of the scale (A, C and E). This is called an A minor (Am) chord.

For the III chord, use the 3, 5 and 7 notes of the scale (B, D and F♯). This is called a B minor (Bm) chord.

For the VI chord, use the 6, 8 and 10 notes of the scale (E, G and B). This is called an E minor (Em) chord.

Here are the easiest forms of the chords discussed above:

II
Am (A-C-E)

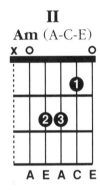

A E A C E

III
Bm (B-D-F♯)

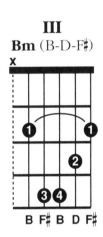

B F♯ B D F♯

VI
Em (E-G-B)

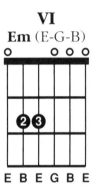

E B E G B E

SUMMARY

The six most common chords in the key of G major are:

The I chord, G major, consisting of the notes G, B and D;

The II chord, A minor, consisting of the notes A, C and E;

The III chord, B minor, consisting of the notes B, D and F♯;

The IV chord, C major, consisting of the notes C, E and G;

The V7 chord, D seventh, consisting of the notes D, F♯, A and C;

The VI chord, E minor, consisting of the notes E, G, and B.

QUESTIONS ABOUT CHORDS

1. What is the I chord in the key of C major? _____ in the key of F major? _____

2. What is the II chord in the key of G major? _____ in the key of C major? _____

3. What is the IV chord in the key of F major? _____ in the key of G major? _____

4. What is the V7 chord in the key of C major? _____ in the key of F major? _____

    in the key of G major? _____

5. What is the VI chord in the key of G major? _____ in the key of F major? _____

    in the key of C major? _____

6. What is the III chord in the key of G major? _____ in the key of F major? _____

    in the key of C major? _____

7. What is the I chord in the key of G major? _____

8. What is the II chord in the key of F major? _____

9. What is the IV chord in the key of C major? _____

10. Fill in the most common chords in C major, F major and G major:

Key	I	II	III	IV	V⁷	VI
C						
F						
G						

Name the notes in the most common chords:

11. C major   _C_   _E_   _G_

12. D minor   ____   ____   ____

13. E minor   ____   ____   ____

14. F major   ____   ____   ____

15. G seventh   ____   ____   ____   ____

16. A minor   ____   ____   ____

17. B minor   ____   ____   ____

18. C seventh   ____   ____   ____   ____

19. D seventh   ____   ____   ____   ____

For answers see page 62.

PLAYING THIRDS ON THE GUITAR

Single note passages are often enhanced by adding another note an interval of a 3rd away.
For example, here is:

a single note passage;   **with a 3rd above;**   **and with a third below.**

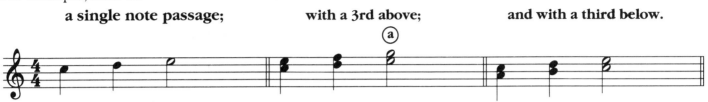

You'll notice at the place marked (a) that the music apparently asks you to play two notes on the same string. Since this is, of course, impossible, you must find the lower note on the next lower string. In other words, the lower note E must be found on the 2nd string. You already know the notes on the first four

frets of the 2nd string: B (open), C (1st fret), C♯ (2nd fret), D (3rd fret) and D♯ (4th fret). Looking at the chromatic wheel on page 28, if necessary, you see that the next note is E, the note we're looking for. It's played on the 2nd string, 5th fret. Therefore, to play the interval E to G, play the G in its normal place, 1st string,

3rd fret, and play the E on the 2nd string, 5th fret.

Using similar reasoning, fill in below where to play the following intervals. Remember, always start with the upper note—then figure out where to play the lower note.

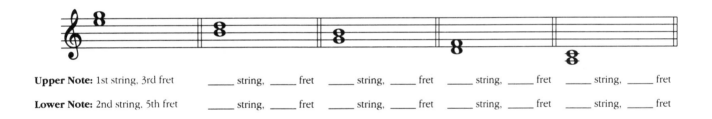

Upper Note: 1st string, 3rd fret   _____ string, _____ fret   _____ string, _____ fret   _____ string, _____ fret   _____ string, _____ fret

Lower Note: 2nd string, 5th fret   _____ string, _____ fret   _____ string, _____ fret   _____ string, _____ fret   _____ string, _____ fret

For answers, see page 62.

Using what you have just learned, you can now play major scales harmonized in thirds.

Follow the fingerings carefully while practicing the note combinations below.

C

F

1st string, 5th fret
2nd string, 6th fret

G

1st string, 5th fret   1st string, 7th fret
2nd string, 7th fret   2nd string, 8th fret

SYNCOPATION

Syncopation is the name given to a musical effect in which a note is anticipated, that is, played before the beat. For example, this rhythm is not syncopated— each quarter note falls in the expected place, *on* the beat.

The following example uses syncopation. The 3rd quarter note is played on the "and" of the 2nd beat, rather than its expected place on the 3rd beat. For best results, count carefully and accent (> = play a little louder) all syncopated notes.

Since the days of ragtime in the late 19th century, syncopation has been an important component in every kind of American music— including Dixieland, swing, rock, blues, country and folk—and is also very important in all of the Latin and Caribbean styles such as rhumba, cha-cha, bossa nova, reggae, ska and salsa. Although a thorough study of syncopation is beyond the scope of this book, the exercises below will introduce you to this essential subject. Serious musicians cannot expect to succeed in popular music without a thorough understanding of syncopation.

Play the following exercises on the open E string. Then when you feel comfortable with the rhythms, make up melodies of your own using the same syncopations.

MINOR SCALES

Minor scales can be derived from the major scales. When a minor scale is derived from a particular major scale, it is called the **relative minor** of that scale or key. For example, the A minor scales are derived from the C major scale, thus the key of A minor is the relative minor key of C major. Conversely, the key of C major is called the **relative major** of the key of A minor.

BUILDING THE A MINOR SCALES

Start with a two-octave C major scale:

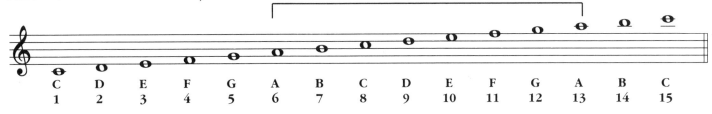

The relative minor scale is always built from the 6th note of the major scale, here the note A. Thus, the A minor scale continues upward with the notes B, C, D, E, F, G and ends on the next A. This is called the A **natural minor scale**.

The A natural minor scale:

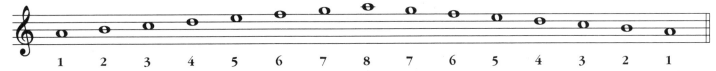

Another type of minor scale is called the **harmonic minor**. This differs from the natural minor because the 7th note is raised a half step.

The A harmonic minor scale:

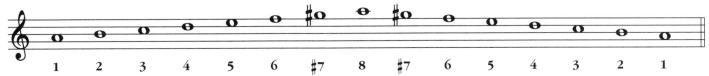

The **melodic minor scale** raises the ascending 6th and 7th notes each by a half step but restores them to the natural notes when descending.

The A melodic minor scale:

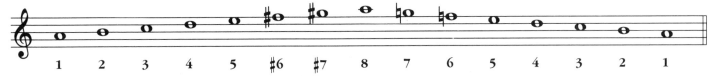

Finally, the **jazz minor scale** raises the 6th and 7th notes each by a half step, ascending and descending.

The A jazz minor scale:

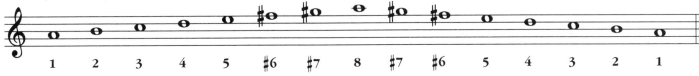

THE THREE PRINCIPAL CHORDS IN THE KEY OF A MINOR

Like the major keys, the three principal chords in the minor keys are also the I, IV and V7 chords. They are derived from the **harmonic minor scale**. Now that you know the A harmonic minor scale, you can derive the three principal chords in the key of A minor. Start with a two-octave A harmonic minor scale:

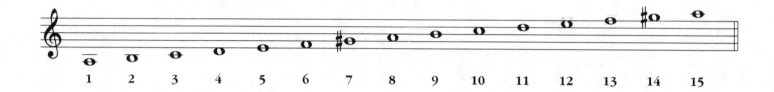

For the I chord, use the 1, 3 and 5 notes of the scale (A, C and E). This is called an A minor (Am) chord.

For the IV chord use the 4, 6 and 8 notes of the scale (D, F and A). This is called a D minor (Dm) chord.

For the V7 chord use the 5, #7, 9 and 11 notes of the scale (E, G#, B and D). This is called an E seventh (E7) chord.

Here are the easiest forms of the chords discussed above:

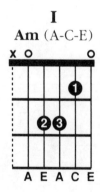

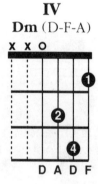

SUMMARY

In the key of A minor, the three pincipal chords are:

The I chord, A minor, consisting of the notes A, C and E;

The IV chord, D minor, consisting of the notes D, F and A;

The V7 chord, E seventh, consisting of the notes E, G#, B and D.

THE E MINOR SCALES

As you have already learned, minor scales are derived from their relative major scale. For example, the relative major to E minor is G major, thus to build the E minor scales you must start with a two-octave G major scale (see page 32). Build the E natural minor scale by using the 6 through 13 notes from the G major scale:

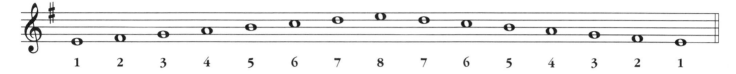

Construct an E harmonic minor scale by using the same notes as the natural minor, but **raise the 7th note by a half step both ascending and descending**.

1.

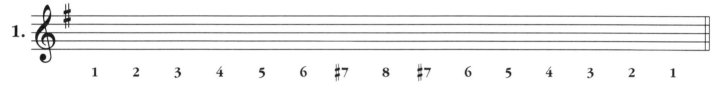

Construct an E melodic minor scale by using the same notes a the natural minor, but **raise the 6th and 7th notes each by a half step ascending, and then restore these notes to naturals when descending**.

2.

Construct an E jazz minor scale by starting with the natural minor scale, then **raise the 6th and 7th notes each by a half step both ascending and descending**.

3.

Using the two-octave E harmonic minor scale below, and the same method we used with the A harmonic minor scale, construct the three principal chords in the key of E minor.

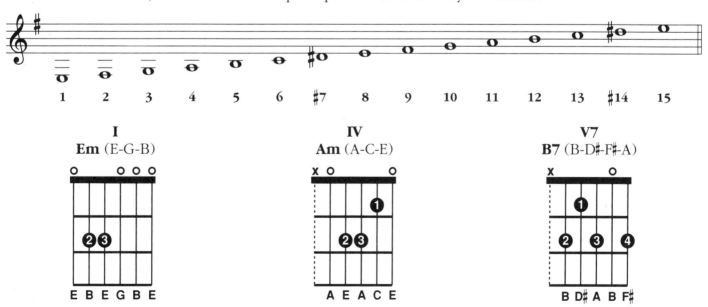

For answers, see page 62.

THE D MINOR SCALES

The D minor scales are derived from their relative major scale, the F major scale. Start with a two-octave F major scale (see page 34). Build the D natural minor scale by using the 6 through 13 notes from the F major scale:

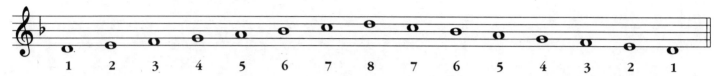

Construct a D harmonic minor scale by writing the natural minor scale, then raising the 7th note by a half step both ascending and descending.

Construct a D melodic minor scale by writing the natural minor scale, raising the 6th and 7th notes each by a half step ascending, and then restoring these notes to naturals when descending.

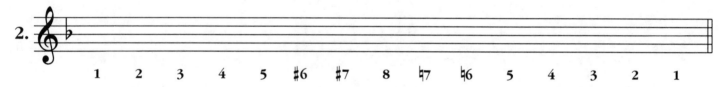

Construct a D jazz minor scale by starting with the natural minor scale, then raising the 6th and 7th notes each by a half step ascending and descending.

Using the two-octave D harmonic minor scale below, and the same method we used with the A harmonic minor scale, construct the three principal chords in the key of D minor.

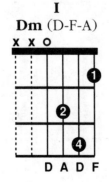

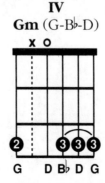

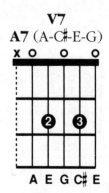

For answers, see page 62.

6/8 TIME

Part I, Slow to Moderate

Because 6/8 time is used to notate two different styles of music, many students are confused about how to play it.

First of all, the "8" in the 6/8 time signature means that, unlike the 2/4, 3/4, and 4/4 you have learned, the 8th note now receives one full beat.

Songs played from a slow to moderate tempo in 6/8 time should be counted "in six," that is, six beats per measure.

Here are some fragments of familiar tunes that should be counted in six:

Drink to Me Only with Thine Eyes

Un Canadien Errant

Nine Men Slept in a Boarding House Bed

Nine men slept in a board-ing house bed, Roll o - ver, roll o - ver...

My Name is Yon Yonson

My name is Yon Yon-son, I come from Vis-con-sin, I vork in the lum-ber mills there...

6/8 TIME

Part II: Moderately Fast to Very Fast

As the tempo of 6/8 time gets faster, it becomes more difficult to count in six. Anything quicker than moderate should be counted "in two." This means that each beat will contain three 8th notes. Put another way, each measure of 6/8 time will contain two groups of three 8th notes each.

Here are some fragments of familiar folk songs and marches in which the 6/8 time should be counted in two:

Pop Goes the Weasel

St. Patrick's Day in the Mornin'

The Liberty Bell

The Farmer in the Dell

BUILDING THE D MAJOR SCALE

First, write the notes from D to D. Make sure neither to skip nor repeat any letter.

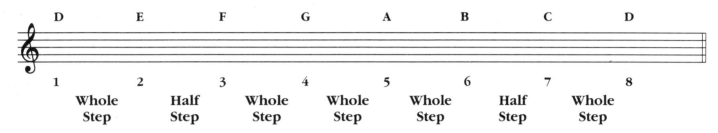

You will remember that the major scale must use these steps:

Whole, whole, half, whole, whole, whole, half (or 2½, 3½).

Check each interval in the scale to make sure that it conforms to this pattern.

1. From the 1st to the 2nd step is a _____ step. It should be a _____ step.

2. From the 2nd to the 3rd step is a _____ step. It should be a _____ step. Therefore, the F must be _____ .

3. From the 3rd to the 4th step is a _____ step. It should be a _____ step.

4. From the 4th to the 5th step is a whole step. It should be a _____ step.

5. From the 5th to the 6th step is a _____ step. It should be a _____ step.

6. From the 6th to the 7th step is a _____ step. It should be a whole step. Therefore, the C must be _____ .

7. From the 7th to the 8th step is a _____ step. It should be a _____ step. This completes the scale.

For answers, see page 62.

Correct Form of the D Major Scale

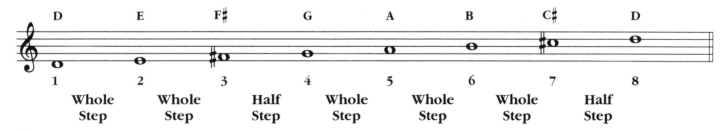

As you can see, the D major scale requires two sharps, F and C.
Ordinarily these are placed in a key signature as follows:

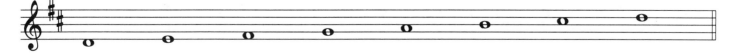

THE THREE PRINCIPAL CHORDS IN THE KEY OF D MAJOR

As you know, the three principal chords in any key are the I, IV and V7 chords. Now that you know the D major scale, you can derive the three principal chords in the key of D major.

Start with a two-octave D major scale:

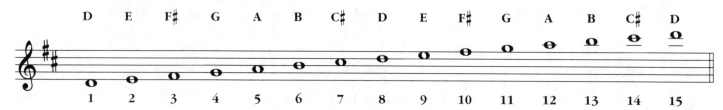

1. The I chord is a D major chord. It consists of the 1, 3 and 5 notes of the scale.

   Write them here. _____ _____ _____

2. The IV chord is a G major chord. It consists of the 4, 6 and 8 notes of the scale.

   Write them here. _____ _____ _____

3. The V7 chord is an A seventh chord. It consists of the 5, 7, 9 and 11 notes of the scale.

   Write them here. _____ _____ _____ _____

For answers, see page 62.

Here are the easiest forms of the chords discussed above:

I	IV	V7
D (D-F♯-A)	**G** (G-B-D)	**A7** (A-C♯-E-G)

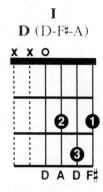

D A D F♯

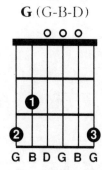

G B D G B G

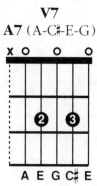

A E G C♯ E

SUMMARY

The three principal chords in the key of D are:

The I chord, D major, consisting of the notes D, F♯ and A;

The IV chord, G major, consisting of the notes G, B and D;

The V7 chord, A seventh, consisting of the notes A, C♯, E and G.

THE DOTTED 8th & 16th NOTE RHYTHM

Like 8th notes, dotted 8ths and 16ths are played two to each beat. But unlike 8th notes (which are played evenly) dotted 8ths and 16ths are played unevenly: long, short, long, short.

Compare the following:

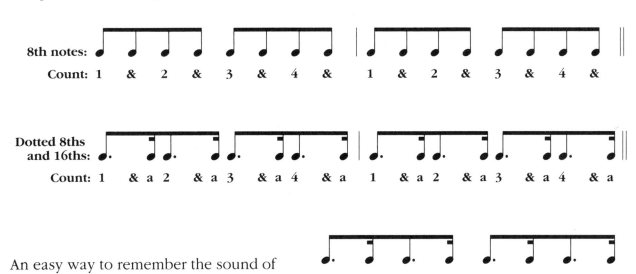

An easy way to remember the sound of dotted 8ths and 16ths is to say the words: "Hump - ty Dump - ty Hump - ty Dump - ty."

Here are some fragments of familiar tunes that will help you remember the sound of the dotted 8th and 16ths:

Down by the Station

Boogie Style

Shall We Gather at the River

TRIPLETS

When three notes are grouped together with the figure "3" above or below the notes, the group is called a **triplet**. The three notes then have a rhythmic value which is the same as two of the same notes. For example, three eighth notes under a triplet sign get the same number of beats as two ordinary eighth notes, or one beat.

Compare the eighth notes and quarter notes in the first line with the triplets in the second line.

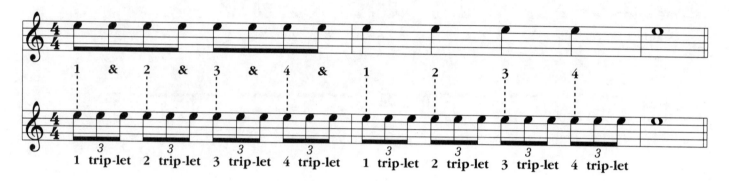

Here are some fragments of familiar tunes that will help you remember the sound of triplets:

Shave and a Haircut

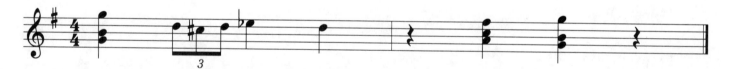

"Triumphal March" from *Aida*

Someone's in the Kitchen with Dinah

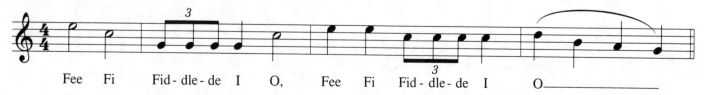

Fee Fi Fid - dle - de I O, Fee Fi Fid - dle - de I O_____

THE CHROMATIC SCALE

The chromatic scale encompasses every note playable on the guitar. Ascending, it is usually written using sharps; descending, flats are used.

Here is a chromatic scale using every note in the first position.

Many modern arrangers write F♯ instead of G♭ even when the passage is descending. Similarly, B♭ is preferred to A♯, and E♭ to D♯. Since the same fingering is used, it's really a matter of convenience, and the well-rounded player will be comfortable with either notation.

A modern way of writing the chromatic scale:

BASIC MUSICAL SYMBOLS RECAP

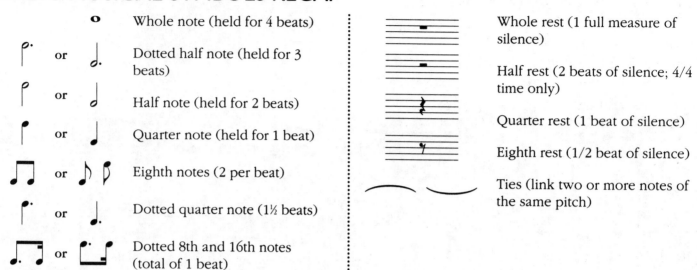

o — Whole note (held for 4 beats)

Dotted half note (held for 3 beats)

Half note (held for 2 beats)

Quarter note (held for 1 beat)

Eighth notes (2 per beat)

Dotted quarter note (1½ beats)

Dotted 8th and 16th notes (total of 1 beat)

Whole rest (1 full measure of silence)

Half rest (2 beats of silence; 4/4 time only)

Quarter rest (1 beat of silence)

Eighth rest (1/2 beat of silence)

Ties (link two or more notes of the same pitch)

Treble clef

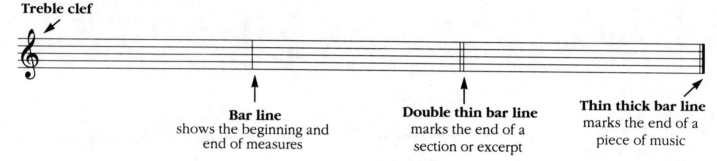

Bar line
shows the beginning and end of measures

Double thin bar line
marks the end of a section or excerpt

Thin thick bar line
marks the end of a piece of music

/ means "repeat preceding chord"

./. means "repeat preceding measure"

.//. means "repeat two preceding measures"

Double repeat signs mean "repeat all the material between the repeat signs"

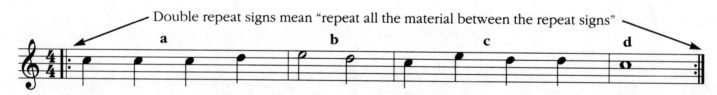

In the example above you would play measures a b c d a b c d.

1st and 2nd endings are used to indicate partial repeats.

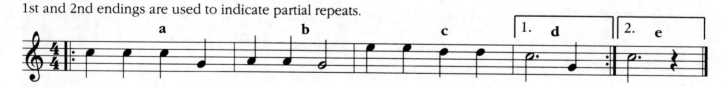

In the example above you would play measures a b c d a b c e.

Key signatures

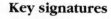

C major
or
A minor

G major
or
E minor

F major
or
D minor

D major
or
B minor

Time signatures

$$\frac{2}{4} \qquad \frac{3}{4} \qquad \frac{4}{4} \qquad \frac{6}{8}$$

Upper number tells you how many beats per measure.
Lower number tells you what kind of note gets one beat.

♯   sharp (raises a note a half step)

♭   flat (lowers a note a half step)

♮   natural (restores a sharped or flatted note to its normal pitch)

8va   abbreviation for the interval of an octave (an 8th)

I, **II**, **III**, **IV**, **V7**, **VI** refer to the chords built on the 1st, 2nd, 3rd, 4th, 5th and 6th notes of a major scale.

MODES

A full discussion of modes is beyond the scope of this book. For our purposes, however, we may basically define modes as different patterns of whole and half steps that comprise a scale. We have seen that the major scale (also known as the Ionian mode) has a pattern of steps of whole, whole, half, whole, whole, whole, half (2½, 3½) and the natural minor scale (also known as the Aeolian mode) has a pattern of 1½, 2½, 2.

Other modes which were used in ancient times have become popular again in the classical works of such composers as Debussy, Bartok and others, and in the rock music of the Beatles, Pink Floyd and many other popular artists.

The examples below use the notes of the C major scale to show the different mode patterns that may be created by building on different notes within the C major scale, and then using those notes as the root upon which you build a new scale. Of course, you may use any major scale as your base scale upon which to build all the various modes, just as you have built various major and minor scales by following the patterns presented earlier in this book.

Ionian mode (this is the major scale)

• pattern: 2½, 3½ steps

• example based on the C major scale: C D E F G A B C

Aeolian mode (starts on the sixth note of the major scale)

• pattern: 1½, 2½, 2 steps

• example based on the C major scale: A B C D E F G A (this is the A natural scale)

• This mode is used in many Celtic folk songs and, for example, "When Johnny Comes Marching Home."

Dorian mode (starts on the second note of the major scale)

• pattern: 1½, 3½, 1 steps

• example based on the C major scale D E F G A B C D

• This mode was used in "Eleanor Rigby" by the Beatles

Phrygian mode (starts on the third note of the major scale)

• pattern ½, 3½, 2 steps

• example based on the C major scale E F G A B C D E

• This mode is the basis for almost all Flamenco music and is probably the reason the guitar is tuned like it is.

Lydian mode (starts on the fourth note of the major scale)

• pattern 3½, 2½ steps

• example based on the C major scale F G A B C D E F

Mixolydian mode (starts on the fifth note of the major scale)

• pattern 2½, 2½, 1 steps

• example based on the C major scale G A B C D E F G

• This mode is used in "Paperback Writer" by the Beatles and the folk song "Old Joe Clarke."

ANSWERS TO PUZZLES AND QUIZZES

Page 7:
1. D F A E C G A D C F E
A G C A D

2. E G B F D E B G D B F
G D E

3. D E F G A B C D E F G
F E D C B A G F E D

4. D F E G C B G E A F D
E F C A G D E B C

Page 8:
1. A BEADED BAG

2. A FADED BADGE

3. A CAB

4. DEAF

5. BAD EGG

6. GABE GABBED

A Limerick

There was a smart monkey
  whose <u>age</u>

Was very hard to <u>gage</u>

He had an old <u>face</u>

But could swing like an <u>ace</u>

From the bottom to the top
  of his <u>cage</u>.

Page 10: There are several possible answers. Here are a few:

Page 12:

Page 23:
1. 2nd string, 2nd fret
   4th string, 3rd fret
   2nd string, 4th fret
   1st string, 2nd fret
   3rd string, 3rd fret
   5th string, 4th fret

2. 1st string open
   5th string, 1st fret
   2nd string, 2nd fret
   2nd string open
   4th string, 1st fret
   4th string, 2nd fret

3. 4th string, 4th fret
   1st string, 5th fret
   4th string, 2nd fret
   1st string, 2nd fret
   2nd string, 2nd fret
   6th string, 5th fret
   2nd string, 3rd fret

4. 1st string, 1st fret
   3rd string open
   2nd string, 1st fret
   4th string open
   4th string, 1st fret
   5th string, 1st fret
   6th string, 1st fret

Page 24:
1. A♯ 3rd string, 3rd fret
   C♯ 2nd string, 2nd fret
   D♯ 4th string, 1st fret
   F♯ 1st string, 2nd fret

2. G♯ 3rd string, 1st fret
   C♯ 5th string, 4th fret
   G♯ 6th string, 4th fret
   G♯ 1st string, 4th fret

3. D♮ 2nd string, 3rd fret
   D♮ 4th string open
   A♮ 1st string, 5th fret
   F♮ 4th string, 3rd fret

4. C♮ 5th string, 3rd fret
   G♮ 1st string, 3rd fret
   F♮ 6th string, 1st fret
   F♮ 1st string, 1st fret

Page 25:
1. A♭ 3rd string, 1st fret
   D♭ 2nd string, 2nd fret
   G♭ 1st string, 2nd fret
   E♭ 4th string, 1st fret

2. A♭ 1st string, 4th fret
   B♭ 5th string, 1st fret
   G♭ 6th string, 2nd fret
   B♭ 1st string, 6th fret

3. E♮ 4th string, 2nd fret
   G♮ 1st string, 3rd fret
   D♮ 2nd string, 3rd fret
   A♮ 3rd string, 2nd fret

4. B♮ 1st string, 7th fret
   G♮ 6th string, 3rd fret
   B♮ 5th string, 2nd fret
   A♮ 1st string, 5th fret

Page 26:

1. D♭ 2nd string, 2nd fret
    A♭ 3rd string, 1st fret
    G♭ 1st string, 2nd fret
    B♭ 3rd string, 3rd fret
    A♭ 1st string, 4th fret
    E♭ 2nd string, 4th fret
    B♭ 1st string, 6th fret
    G♭ 4th string, 4th fret

2. D♭ 5th string, 4th fret
    E♭ 4th string, 1st fret
    B♭ 5th string, 1st fret
    G♭ 6th string, 2nd fret
    A♭ 6th string, 4th fret
    D♭ 5th string, 4th fret
    G♭ 4th string, 4th fret
    G♭ 1st string, 2nd fret

Page 27:

Page 29:

Page 30:

1. whole step, half step, whole, whole, whole, half, whole

2. whole, half, whole, whole, half, whole, whole

3. whole, whole, whole, half, whole, whole, half

4. half, whole, whole, whole, half, whole, whole

None of the above represent major scales. Actually:

1. is in the Dorian mode;
2. is in the Aeolian mode;
3. is in the Lydian mode;
4. is in the Phrygian mode.

For a discussion about modes, see page 59.

Page 39:

1. 2nd, 3rd, 5th, 7th, 4th, 6th

2. 8va, 2nd, 5th, 3rd, 4th, 7th

3. 6th, 4th, 7th, 5th, 3rd, 8va

4. 7th, 4th, 3rd, 5th, 2nd, 8va

5.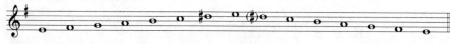
2nd   8va   3rd   7th   5th   4th

6.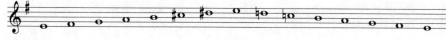
6th   3rd   2nd   5th   5th   6th

7.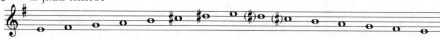
8va   2nd   6th   4th   7th   3rd

8.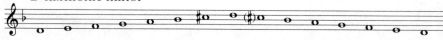
5th   4th   7th   3rd   2nd   8va

Page 40:

1. 2nd, 3rd, 5th, 7th, 4th, 6th
2. 8va, 2nd, 5th, 3rd, 4th, 7th
3. 6th, 4th, 6th, 5th, 3rd, 8va
4. 7th, 4th, 3rd, 5th, 2nd, 8va
5. 3rd, 2nd, 7th, 4th, 6th, 2nd
6. 4th, 5th, 6th, 3rd, 7th, 2nd
7. 8va, 3rd, 2nd, 2nd, 7th, 4th
8. 6th, 5th, 8va, 2nd, 6th, 8va

Page 44:
1. C, F
2. Am, Dm
3. B♭, C
4. G7, C7, D7
5. Em, Dm, Am
6. Bm, Am, Em
7. G
8. Gm
9. F

10.

Key	I	II	III	IV	V⁷	VI
C	C	Dm	Em	F	G⁷	Am
F	F	Gm	Am	B♭	C⁷	Dm
G	G	Am	Bm	C	D⁷	Em

11. C E G
12. D F A
13. E G B
14. F A C
15. G B D F
16. A C E
17. B D F♯
18. C E G B♭
19. D F♯ A C

Page 45:

Upper note:
1st string, 3rd fret;
2nd string, 3rd fret
2nd string open
4th string, 3rd fret
5th string, 3rd fret

Lower note:
1st string, 5th fret
3rd string, 4th fret
3rd string open
5th string, 5th fret
6th string, 5th fret

Page 49:

1. E harmonic minor
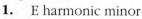

2. E melodic minor

3. E jazz minor

Page 50:

1. D harmonic minor

2. D melodic minor

3. D jazz minor

Page 53:

1. whole, whole
2. half, whole, sharped
3. half, half
4. whole
5. whole, whole
6. half, sharped
7. half, half

Page 54:

1. D F♯ A
2. G B D
3. A C♯ E G

INDEX

Guitar Fingerboard Chart
Frets 1–12

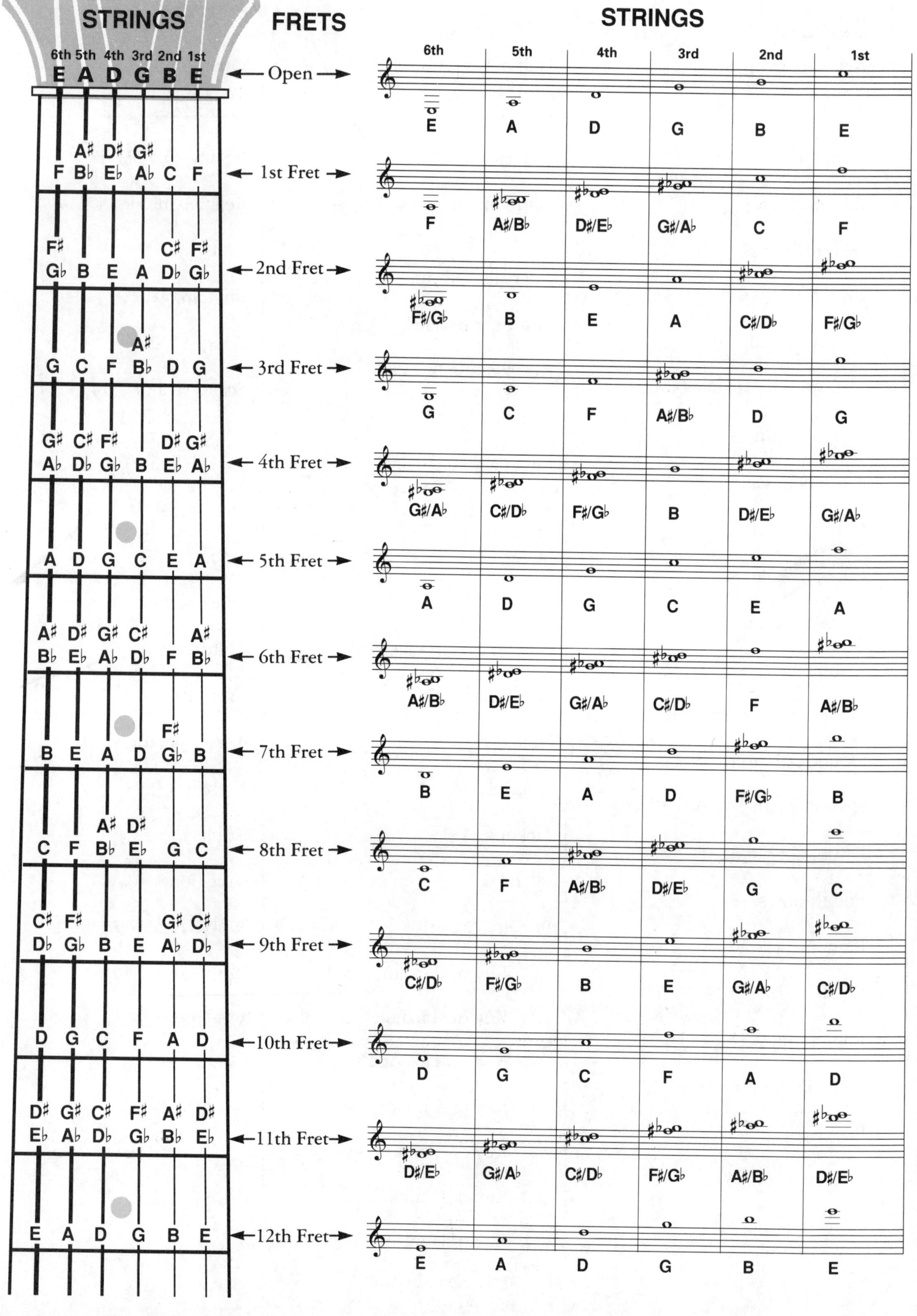

STRINGS | **FRETS** | **STRINGS**

6th	5th	4th	3rd	2nd	1st

Fretboard diagram (left):

Fret	6th	5th	4th	3rd	2nd	1st
Open	E	A	D	G	B	E
1st Fret	F	A#/Bb	D#/Eb	G#/Ab	C	F
2nd Fret	F#/Gb	B	E	A	C#/Db	F#/Gb
3rd Fret	G	C	F	A#/Bb	D	G
4th Fret	G#/Ab	C#/Db	F#/Gb	B	D#/Eb	G#/Ab
5th Fret	A	D	G	C	E	A
6th Fret	A#/Bb	D#/Eb	G#/Ab	C#/Db	F	A#/Bb
7th Fret	B	E	A	D	F#/Gb	B
8th Fret	C	F	A#/Bb	D#/Eb	G	C
9th Fret	C#/Db	F#/Gb	B	E	G#/Ab	C#/Db
10th Fret	D	G	C	F	A	D
11th Fret	D#/Eb	G#/Ab	C#/Db	F#/Gb	A#/Bb	D#/Eb
12th Fret	E	A	D	G	B	E

Staff notation (right side) — string note names per fret:

	6th	5th	4th	3rd	2nd	1st
Open	E	A	D	G	B	E
1st	F	A#/Bb	D#/Eb	G#/Ab	C	F
2nd	F#/Gb	B	E	A	C#/Db	F#/Gb
3rd	G	C	F	A#/Bb	D	G
4th	G#/Ab	C#/Db	F#/Gb	B	D#/Eb	G#/Ab
5th	A	D	G	C	E	A
6th	A#/Bb	D#/Eb	G#/Ab	C#/Db	F	A#/Bb
7th	B	E	A	D	F#/Gb	B
8th	C	F	A#/Bb	D#/Eb	G	C
9th	C#/Db	F#/Gb	B	E	G#/Ab	C#/Db
10th	D	G	C	F	A	D
11th	D#/Eb	G#/Ab	C#/Db	F#/Gb	A#/Bb	D#/Eb
12th	E	A	D	G	B	E